D1580204

THE HP SAUCE COOKBOOK

HP
SAUCE
THE Original

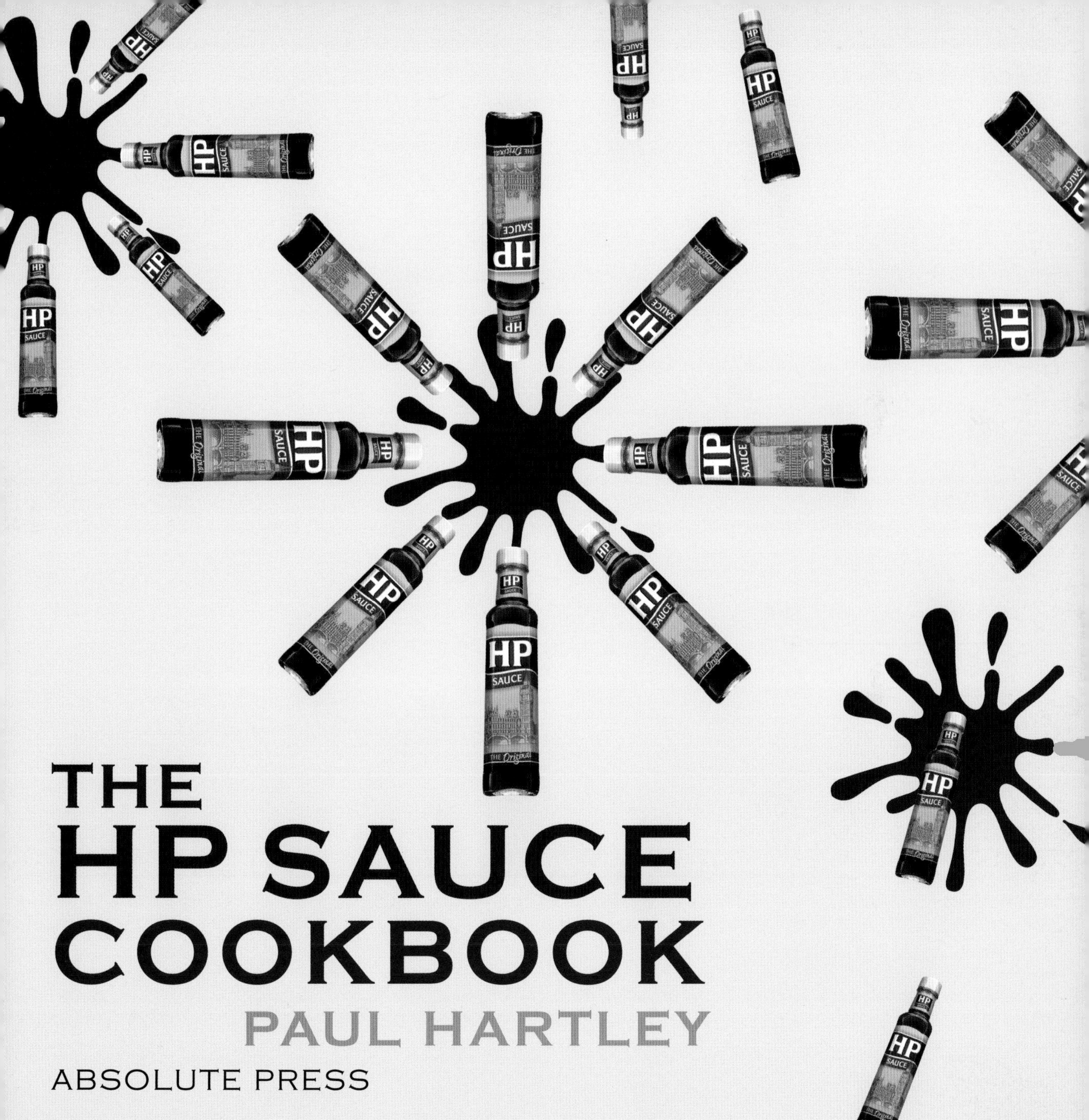

THE HP SAUCE COOKBOOK

PAUL HARTLEY

ABSOLUTE PRESS

In association with
www.breakfastandbrunch.com

First published in Great Britain in 2008
by **Absolute Press**
Scarborough House
29 James Street West
Bath BA1 2BT England
Phone 44 (0) 1225 316013
Fax 44 (0) 1225 445836
E-mail info@absolutepress.co.uk
Website www.absolutepress.co.uk

Publisher
Jon Croft
Commissioning Editor
Meg Avent
Designer
Matt Inwood
Design Assistant
Claire Siggery
Publishing Assistant
Andrea O' Connor
Photography
David Loftus
Props Stylist
Liz Belton
Food Stylist
Trish Hilferty

Reprinted 2009

A catalogue record of this book is available from the British Library

ISBN 9781904573869

Printed in China on behalf of Latitude Press Limited

CONTENTS

A BRIEF HISTORY... 6

SCALLOP, CHORIZO & WARM POTATO SALAD 10
TUSCAN THREE MEAT STEW 11
COUSCOUS-STUFFED PEPPERS 12
GRILLED TUNA WITH HP LIME MARINADE 15
THE GREAT BRITISH SAUSAGE SANDWICH 16
HOT TAMARIND CHICKEN 18
BACON & SWEETCORN FRITTERS 19
SLOW-COOKED BARBECUE PORK BELLY 20
WELSH RAREBIT... THE HP WAY 23
HP KING DUCK 25
KING PRAWN PATIA WITH MUSCOVADO & YOGHURT 26
PEACH-GLAZED PORK FILLET 28
DELUXE STEAK BURGERS 29
DEEP VEGETABLE AND HP PIE 30
CRAB CLAWS WITH GINGER & CORIANDER 32
LAMB & MINT PASTIES 35
PHEASANT WITH DATE & RED WINE SAUCE 38
GUJERATI MANGO & LENTIL CURRY 39
BRUNCH WRAP 41
CALF'S LIVER & PANCETTA WITH CARAMELISED RED ONIONS 42
MIDDLE EASTERN HOT PEPPER DIP 43
OXTAIL SOUP 44
SINGAPORE PEANUT NOODLES 45
CHEESY TORTILLAS WITH RATATOUILLE 48
HP STEAK & MUSHROOM JACKETS 51
BRISKET WITH FIGS & RUM 52
HUNTERS' CHICKEN 53
ROAST POUSSIN WITH GARLIC & HERBS 55
MAPLE HP RIB CHOPS 56
STUFFED BUTTERNUT SQUASH 57
HONEY-GRILLED SALMON WITH KIWI & CUCUMBER SALSA 61
LAMB TAGINE WITH PRUNES, OLIVES & ALMONDS 62
BEEF ON THE BONE WITH CHOP HOUSE BUTTER 63
FLORENTINE PASTA 64
VENISON TARTARE 65
DEVILLED LAMB & APRICOT KEBABS 66
MULLIGATAWNY SOUP 69
SPICY ORIENTAL LETTUCE SHELLS 70
SHEPHERD'S PIE 71
MEXICAN BEEF AND BEAN WRAPS 74

ACKNOWLEDGEMENTS 78

IN THE BEGINNING... THERE WAS A SAUCE, AND THE SAUCE TASTED GOOD....

A BRIEF HISTORY... FROM 'BREWERY SET-UPS' TO 'KNOCKOUT PUNCHES'

Over the next seventy-or-so pages runs the story of some landmark moments from the history of a brown sauce that established itself as a household name and a national icon. It starts with the humble beginnings of a Midlands brewery business. Then there are tales of how a simple, world-beating recipe was found and purchased; how a name was arrived at and a link to Parliament was formed; how a glorious new addition to the kitchen storecupboard was launched; how a basic education in French was gifted to children the country over; how a Prime Minister became forever inextricably connected with a sauce he never claimed to have loved; and how the irritable heavyweight boxing champion of the world could be placated when served his evening meal. It's a piquant little story that we'll tell over these panels through the pages of this book. **READ ON p10**

THE HP SAUCE RECIPE COLLECTION

HP®
SAUCE
HP®
SAUCE

SCALLOP, CHORIZO & WARM POTATO SALAD

The fusion of sea-fresh scallops sautéed with chorizo and served with a warm potato salad is extraordinarily good. The HP Sauce enhances all the flavours.

SERVES 2

300g potatoes, peeled and cooked
4 tablespoons mayonnaise
2 teaspoons olive oil
1 teaspoon malt vinegar
1 heaped teaspoon chopped chives
pinch of salt
25g unsalted butter
2 tablespoons HP Sauce
2 tablespoons fresh lemon juice
freshly ground black pepper
8 king scallops
50g chorizo, diced into 1cm bits
smoked paprika

Slice the potatoes while still warm in half and then cut them into $^1/_2$cm slices.

In a bowl mix the mayonnaise with the olive oil, vinegar, chives and salt then add the potatoes and carefully mix them together. Set aside and keep warm.

In a frying pan melt the butter and then add the HP Sauce, lemon juice and black pepper. Now add the scallops over a medium heat and roll them in the juices. They will need about 2–3 minutes on each side basting as they cook. Add the chorizo and cook until warmed through. It will go hard if cooked too long.

Spoon a helping of warm potato salad onto a plate and make a nest in the centre. Place the scallop and chorizo mixture in the middle, dust with smoked paprika and serve.

It was in 1875 that an ambitious young man arrived in the manor of Aston to establish the Midland Vinegar Company. Edwin Samson Moore knew that labour, in this part of the Midlands, was cheap and that the water in the area was hard – essential for the brewing of

TUSCAN THREE MEAT STEW

My good friend and restaurateur, Roberto, introduced me to this long slow-cook recipe. A recipe inspired by his culinary expertise that encapsulated the flavour of Tuscany.

SERVES 8

2 tablespoons olive oil
300g shallots, peeled and roughly chopped
5 cloves garlic, finely diced
6 stems celery, diced
1 teaspoon dried thyme
1 teaspoon freshly chopped rosemary
6 bay leaves
500g diced pork
500g diced lamb
500g diced braising steak
$^{1}/_{4}$ teaspoon salt
lots of freshly ground black pepper
400g tin chopped tomatoes
2 tablespoons tomato purée
3 tablespoons HP Sauce
150g pitted green olives
1 bottle Italian red wine

Heat the olive oil in a large flameproof casserole and add the shallots, garlic, celery and herbs. Sauté gently for 5–6 minutes and then add in the meats.

Brown the meat all over for a further 5 minutes letting the juices run and then season with the salt and pepper. Add all the remaining ingredients to the casserole, stir well to combine and put the casserole in the oven at 70C/150F/Gas $^{1}/_{4}$ for 3 hours.

After 3 hours remove the lid of the casserole, stir the stew gently and return to the oven uncovered for a further 2 hours so that the liquid reduces and you have a deliciously rich stew with thick gravy.

Serve traditionally with papardelle pasta and a crunchy green salad.

vinegar. Moore's cousin invested in the business, which helped to provide a stable platform from which the company could grow and rival the other vinegar brewers in the area. Potato chips from France had just taken the country by storm and it became all the rage to partner them with fried fish. Moore probably didn't know that a national culinary institution was in the improved the dish beyond doubt. Vinegar was a blossoming industry. The business prospered. Moore's eldest son, Edwin, joined the firm in 1890, and as the century drew to a close, a man of less ambition might have been forgiven for being very satisfied with his lot in life. But not so Moore the Elder, for he had a much bigger dream. **READ ON... p18**

COUSCOUS-STUFFED PEPPERS

The fully flavoured couscous encased in these sweet roasted peppers makes a great dish on its own or as an accompaniment to grilled fish.

SERVES 2

2 red peppers
salt and pepper
150g of mixed antipasti in olive oil
100g couscous
125ml vegetable stock
1 onion, peeled and chopped
1 clove garlic, peeled and crushed
4 cherry tomatoes, roughly chopped
2 tablespoons HP Sauce
200g Feta cheese, crumbled
fresh torn basil leaves

Preheat the oven to 180C/350F/Gas 4.

Cut the peppers in half lengthways and remove the seeds. Brush them all over with a little oil from the antipasto, lay them in a baking dish and season with salt and pepper. Roast in the oven for 15 minutes.

Put the couscous into a bowl and add hot vegetable stock. Leave to stand for 5 minutes and then fluff it up with a fork. Using a little more oil from the antipasti fry the onion and garlic until softened and then add the cherry tomatoes and HP Sauce and cook for a couple of minutes.

Tip the onion mixture into the couscous, add the diced mixed antipasto and the crumbled Feta and stir the whole lot together. Remove the peppers from the oven and pack in the couscous mixture so that it is mounded. Return them to the oven for a further 15 minutes until the topping is golden.

Serve with a scattering of basil, a mixed leafy salad and a good dollop of minted yoghurt.

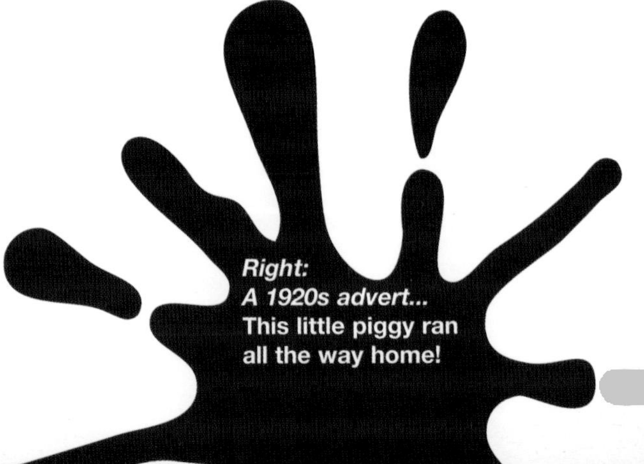

Right:
A 1920s advert...
This little piggy ran all the way home!

H.P. SAUCE
Good with bacon
GARTON'S
H.P.
SAUCE
COPYRIGHT

H.P.
SAUCE
"NO SCRAPS
FOR US NOW THEY USE
H.P. SAUCE."

GRILLED TUNA WITH HP LIME MARINADE

You can serve this with handmade chips for a great alternative take on fish and chips. The HP Sauce fused with the fresh lime juice is just a terrific combination with fresh tuna.

SERVES 4

4 fresh tuna steaks
5 tablespoons lime juice
3 tablespoons HP Sauce
4 spring onions
25g sesame seeds, toasted

Lay the tuna steaks in a shallow dish, mix together the lime juice and HP Sauce and pour it over them. Leave in the fridge to marinate for 2 hours.

Trim off any tired ends of the spring onion leaves and cut off the root. Working up from the root 'end' slice the leaves off at about 8cm and set aside the spare green tops, finely sliced into matchstick lengths.

Take the white part of the spring onion and starting 2cm in from the root end using a small sharp knife make a cut through up to the other end. Rotate the spring onion and repeat until you have made half a dozen cuts and the feathery slithers of the spring onion have opened up. Put them into ice-cold water and leave in the fridge for 1 hour when they will have formed pretty curls.

Set the grill to medium high and cook the tuna steaks for 2–3 minutes on each side, all the time basting with the marinade. Serve sprinkled with toasted sesame seeds and the reserved sliced green onion tops. Remove the spring onions from the water, drain on kitchen paper and arrange on top of the tuna.

Finish with a drizzle of the marinade juice around the plate and a few handmade chips.

Left
A 1930s advert...
Making scraps a thing of the past!

THE GREAT BRITISH SAUSAGE SANDWICH

One of England's finest culinary traditions is the sausage sandwich. This scrummy combination will keep the troops happy at any time of the day.

MAKES 4 SANDWICHES

8 slices granary or sourdough bread
butter
wholegrain mustard
HP Sauce
4 large sausages
piccalilli
2–3 sliced tomatoes

Cook the sausages for 12–15 minutes and keep warm.

Spread each slice of bread with butter, then spread 4 of the slices with mustard and 4 with HP Sauce.

Cut each sausage into 3 slices lengthways and place on top of the mustard coated bread. Add a generous dollop of piccalilli and cover with tomato slices.

Top with the HP bread slices, cut in half and serve to a delighted audience

HOT TAMARIND CHICKEN

This is an exotic chicken dish infused with chillies, peppers, garlic and vivacious tamarind creating a hot and slightly sour dish that will make your taste buds dance with delight.

SERVES 2

2 free range chicken breasts
1 tablespoon HP Sauce
1 teaspoon tamarind paste
½ teaspoon sea salt
1 tablespoon vegetable oil
1 onion, chopped
2 cloves garlic, finely diced
1 stalk lemongrass, finely sliced
1 green pepper, deseeded and sliced
4 green chillies, deseeded and finely diced
1 tomato, roughly chopped
4 kaffir lime leaves, crumbled

Cut 3 shallow slits in each chicken breast. Mix together the HP, tamarind and salt and spread this over the meat and into the slits. Cover and leave to marinate for 1 hour.

Heat the vegetable oil in a frying pan and add the onion and garlic. Fry for 3–4 minutes. Reduce to a low heat and add in the lemongrass, pepper, chillies and tomatoes and cook for a further 5 minutes, moving the mixture gently around the pan.

Now nestle the marinated chicken breasts cut side down, together with any remaining marinade, into the mixture, add the lime leaves and 150ml of water, cover and simmer very gently for 30 minutes turning the chicken once. Add a little more water if needed and spoon the mixture over the chicken from time to time. Remove the lid for the last 5 minutes to reduce the liquid.

A CANCELLED DEBT AND A HANDSOME PROCUREMENT

Whilst driven to expanding the Midland Vinegar Company inventory in new and exciting ways, Moore also had to busy himself with some of the more everyday demands of running a business. Amongst

BACON & SWEETCORN FRITTERS

Brighten up breakfast and brunch with these delicious quick and easy to cook fritters.

FOR 4 PEOPLE

100g self-raising flour
4 tablespoons milk
$^1/_2$ teaspoon baking powder
1 free range egg, beaten
2 tablespoons HP Sauce
325g tin of sweetcorn kernels
6 rashers back bacon, grilled and diced
vegetable oil for frying
maple syrup to serve

Make a stiff batter by putting the sieved flour and baking powder into a bowl, make a well in the centre for the egg and gradually add the milk. Beat well and then add the HP Sauce and beat for a further minute. Fold in the drained sweetcorn and diced bacon so that they are well mixed with the batter and refrigerate for 20 minutes.

Oil a griddle or heavy frying pan over a medium-high heat and spoon on tablespoons of the mixture. Cook for 2–3 minutes, turning once, until golden brown. Continue until all the mixture is used and then serve in stacks drizzled with maple syrup.

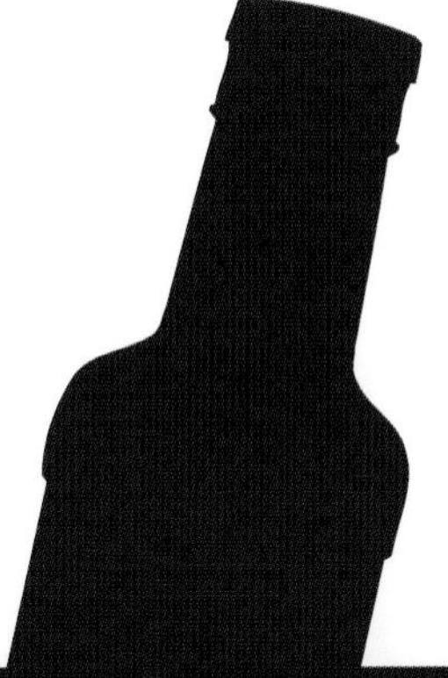

these more mundane requirements was the chasing up of accounts that had fallen into arrears. One such account was with a grocer by the name of Mr F. G. Garton. Moore and son visited the grocer personally to see if they might succeed in settling the debt. They introduced themselves to Mr Garton and removed themselves to an area behind the shop that would allow for discretion. There they were greeted by the most heavenly smell emanating from a copper which contained a rich, exotic-looking sauce. It tasted no less wonderful than it smelled and Moore realised immediately that he had stumbled upon something quite special; the very thing which would fulfil his most ardent business dream. There was then just one other small matter that was to delay by mere seconds the cancellation of Mr Garton's bad debt and the offering of £150 for the purchase of the grocer's piquant sauce recipe. That small matter was the detail of a name.

READ ON... p28

SLOW-COOKED BARBECUE PORK BELLY

This is just the most delicious and succulent pork you will ever eat – tender, aromatic and packed with flavour.

SERVES 6–8
FOR A BARBECUE PARTY

2kg pork belly, prepared in 1 piece
1 litre Coca-Cola
½ teaspoon freshly chopped ginger
3 whole cloves
1 cinnamon stick (about 10cm long)
3 star anise

For the marinade
200g soft dark brown sugar
300ml malt vinegar
½ teaspoon ground cinnamon
½ teaspoon ground allspice
4 tablespoons HP Sauce
2 heaped teaspoons horseradish sauce
200ml dark rum
fresh coriander to garnish

Preheat the oven to 150C/300F/Gas 2.

Put the pork belly into a suitable size deep ovenproof dish to lay it out flat. In a saucepan put the Coca-Cola, ginger, cloves, cinnamon and star anise and bring to the boil. Simmer for 10 minutes and then pour over the pork. Cook in the oven for 2½ hours by which time the meat should be very tender.

Lift out the pork, drain and discard the liquid, and leave aside to cool in the dish.

Now make the marinade. Put the sugar, vinegar, cinnamon and allspice into a pan and bring to the boil. Turn down the heat and keep cooking until the liquid has reduced by half. Remove from the heat and stir in the HP Sauce, horseradish and rum. Let the marinade cool before pouring it over the pork belly. Put in the fridge covered with clingfilm to infuse for 3–4 hours.

Time to fire up the barbie or, if the clouds roll in, heat the grill to medium high. Arrange the pork over the hot coals, preferably with the lid down for it to take on the delicious smokiness, and cook for 10 minutes or until it is heated totally through. To serve, slice up the tender pork and scatter with freshly chopped coriander.

"What is the

4TH CONDIMENT?"

"Why haven't I been introduced to this 4th Condiment?" asked the Knife.

"Don't be silly," cried the Mustard hotly, "you know him as well as you know Salt, Pepper and myself. He's one of the most active members of the League of Condiments. Where will you find such a one for flavour as H.P. Sauce?"

"H.P. Sauce!" exclaimed the Knife, "I say, I can't be very sharp this morning. None of you fellows keep me busier than that most appetising of all sauces."

H P SAUCE

of course!

and only 9d. the bottle!

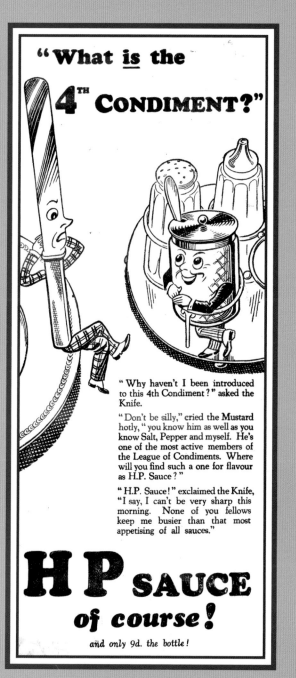

Left
From the 1930s...
In celebrated tabletop company!

Everything goes with

SAUCE

WELSH RAREBIT... THE HP WAY

Just try this and you'll see the difference that HP Sauce makes – it really adds extra flavour and makes this into a great lunchtime treat.

FOR 4 PEOPLE

50ml traditional ale
1 tablespoon HP Sauce
1 teaspoon prepared English mustard
1 teaspoon dry English mustard
$^{1}/_{4}$ teaspoon cayenne pepper
300g mature Cheddar cheese, grated
1 ciabatta loaf
pinch of paprika
mixed leaves to serve

Put the beer, HP Sauce, mustards and cayenne in a pan and bring to a simmer. Remove from the stove and add the grated cheese, a little at a time, until you have the consistency of porridge.

Cut the ciabatta in half and then split each half and toast lightly. Spoon the cheesy mixture over the 4 ciabatta pieces and sprinkle the tops with paprika.

Place under a hot grill until bubbling with golden flecks. Serve each rarebit topped with a handful of mixed leaves.

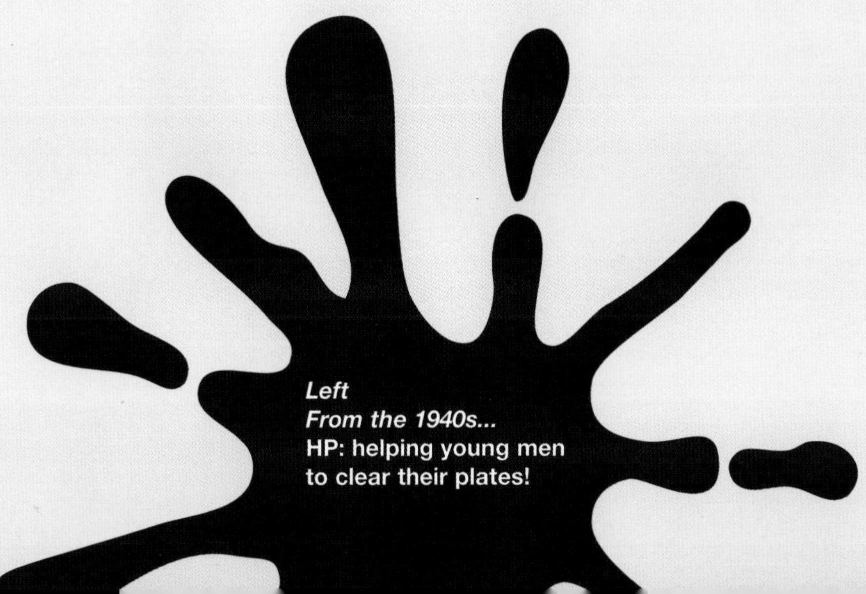

Left
From the 1940s...
HP: helping young men to clear their plates!

HP KING DUCK

This famous Oriental classic presented my way absorbs all the wonderful flavours you would expect but with a twist.

SERVES 4

For the pancakes
125g self-raising flour
$^1/_2$ tsp salt
1 medium free range egg, beaten
25g butter, melted
150ml milk
vegetable oil for frying

$^1/_2$ small cucumber
4 spring onions, white and green parts
4 tablespoons HP Sauce
1 tablespoon runny honey, plus extra for brushing
$^1/_4$ teaspoon Chinese five-spice powder
1 teaspoon redcurrant jelly
1 tablespoon dark soy sauce
2 duck breasts
salt
sesame oil for frying

First prepare the pancake batter. Mix the sieved flour with the salt. Gradually whisk in the egg, butter and milk to form a smooth thick batter. Chill for 30 minutes.

Slice the cucumber into 4cm chunks. Take each chunk and cut into thin matchstick strips. Top and tail the spring onions, cut into 4cm pieces and slice each piece into fine shreds. Set aside. Mix together the HP, honey, spice powder, redcurrant jelly and soy in a small bowl, making sure the jelly is well dispersed and leave until ready to serve.

Heat a little oil in a frying pan and add 1 tablespoon of the batter. Spread it out with the back of a spoon until you have about an 8cm round. Gently cook for 1–2 minutes until bubbles surface. Flip over and cook for another minute. You want to achieve thin crispy pancakes. Repeat to make 8 small pancakes. (You will probably have some batter left over for seconds!)

Put the duck breasts into a shallow dish and pour boiling water over the skin. This will help it crisp when cooking. Drain and pat dry with kitchen paper. Season the skin with a little salt. Heat a heavy based pan with a small amount of sesame oil. Put the duck breasts in over a medium to high heat skin side down to crisp and cook for 5 minutes. Reduce the heat, turn the duck over and cook for 5–6 minutes for pink or longer for well done. While the flesh side is cooking brush honey over the skin side. Remove the duck breasts and leave to rest for 5 minutes, then cut into thin diagonal slices.

For each person take 1 pancake, lay on some duck slices, drizzle with the sauce then lay on some cucumber, then some spring onion. Repeat the process with a second pancake.

KING PRAWN PATIA WITH MUSCOVADO & YOGHURT

This looks tricky but is actually ridiculously easy!

SERVES 4

4 tablespoons natural yoghurt
1 medium onion, chopped
2 cloves garlic
3cm piece of fresh ginger, peeled and diced
1 teaspoon coriander seeds
1 teaspoon cumin seeds
1 teaspoon black mustard seeds
2 tablespoons vegetable oil
2 teaspoons paprika
$\frac{1}{2}$ teaspoon cayenne
$\frac{1}{2}$ teaspoon turmeric
2 tablespoons light muscovado sugar
1 tablespoon white wine vinegar
2 tablespoons tomato purée
2 tablespoons HP Sauce
500g peeled king prawns

Put the yoghurt, onion, garlic and ginger into a blender and blitz with 3 tablespoons of water to make a paste.

In a hot frying pan or wok dry roast the coriander, cumin and black mustard seeds until they start to pop – about 20–30 seconds – and then crush them lightly in a pestle and mortar to release the flavours. Return the pan to the heat add the oil, the crushed spices, paprika, cayenne and turmeric and cook very gently for 2 minutes, being careful not to burn the spices.

Add the yoghurt paste to the pan of spices and fry gently for 8–10 minutes, stirring from time to time until the mixture turns a golden colour. While this is cooking mix together the sugar, vinegar, tomato purée and HP Sauce and pour it into the pan to make a fairly thick mixture. Add a splash of water if it is too thick and simmer gently for 5 minutes.

Toss in the prawns, season with a little salt if required, and cook just long enough to heat the prawns through without overcooking them. You should have a thick, 'grainy' sauce that will coat the prawns perfectly. Serve on a bed of jasmine rice.

Right
A c.1930s advert....
A sauce for celebration!

GARTON'S
H.P.
SAUCE
GARTON'S
SAUCE
FRUITS
MALT VINEGAR

PEACH-GLAZED PORK FILLET

The spices and fruit from the HP Sauce marry wonderfully with the peach conserve to give this pork tenderloin dish oodles of flavour.

SERVES 2

300g pork tenderloin, sliced into 1cm-thick medallions
salt and pepper
3 tablespoons peach conserve
2 tablespoons HP Sauce
1 tablespoon balsamic vinegar
1/4 teaspoon ground cumin
chopped parsley

Season the pork medallions with salt and pepper.

Melt the peach conserve in a pan by mashing any fruit pieces and add the HP sauce, balsamic vinegar, cumin and a good grind of black pepper and stir them all together. Allow to cool and then pour over the pork medallions. Leave to marinate for 1 hour.

Line a grill rack with foil and heat the grill to medium. Using some tongs remove the pork from the marinade and lay out the medallions on the grill pan. Baste with plenty of the marinade and grill for 8–10 minutes, turning and basting as it cooks.

Serve scattered with chopped parsley or coriander.

HOUSES OF PARLIAMENT SAUCE

Moore knew that finding his sauce was one thing, but finding the right name was quite another. He wanted to manufacture a sauce that would win the affections of a nation and become a household name for years and

DELUXE STEAK BURGERS

Good burgers are so versatile; serve them with red onion gravy, roast sweet potato wedges, grilled asparagus or a simple salad.

MAKES 6 BURGERS

650g best lean minced rump steak
2 rashers unsmoked back bacon, diced
1 medium onion, finely diced
1 clove garlic, finely diced
1 medium free range egg
1 teaspoon anchovy essence
2 tablespoons HP Sauce
$^1/_2$ teaspoon dried thyme
$^1/_2$ teaspoon dried sage
pinch of salt
freshly ground black pepper
1 tablespoon plain flour
olive oil

Place all the ingredients, except the flour and oil, into a large mixing bowl and combine together. You can use a wooden spoon but your hands will do the job much better. Add the flour and work it in evenly to help bind the mixture.

Divide the mixture into 6 equal patties making sure you squeeze each one quite firmly to make a good solid burger.

Place the burgers onto greaseproof paper and pop into the fridge for about an hour. You can leave them longer but the idea is to get the mixture to set so that they stay in good shape while cooking.

Heat about 1 tablespoon of olive oil in a frying pan or griddle (or brushed onto a barbecue) and when the oil is hot pop in (or on) the burgers. Cook them for 5–8 minutes and turn over for another 5–8 minutes.

years to come. Serendipity had led Moore and son to within smelling distance of Mr Garton's brew, but perhaps he believed it was fate when Moore was gifted with the most apt of names for the grocer's concoction. Through an open door his gaze landed upon the cart which Garton used to transport his goods to customers. Propped there, against the spokes of one wheel, was a board with thick painted words exclaiming GARTON'S HP SAUCE! A fittingly snappy appellation, he didn't doubt, but, 'Why the letters HP?', Moore asked of the grocer. Rumour had it, revealed Garton, that a bottle of his sauce had been spotted at one of the restaurants of the Houses of Parliament! Goodness gracious – could there be a more apt symbol to win over the British nation? Moore was intoxicated with joy. He had found his sauce, he had found its name; he didn't doubt it would find the people, it was now all just a question of timing. **READ ON... p38**

DEEP VEGETABLE AND HP PIE

This is a classic layered vegetable terrine infused with cream and HP Sauce. It can be served hot or cut into slices and served cold – great picnic food.

SERVES 4–6

$\frac{1}{2}$ tablespoon olive oil
1 large potato, peeled and very thinly sliced
1 medium aubergine, skin on and cut into $\frac{1}{2}$cm slices
1 leek, washed and very thinly sliced
2 medium courgettes, skin on and cut into $\frac{1}{2}$cm rings
salt and black pepper
1 clove garlic finely diced
mixed dried herbs
350ml double cream
3 tablespoons HP Sauce
$1\frac{1}{2}$ leaves gelatine

You will need an ovenproof dish about 25cm x 20cm.

Preheat the over to 180C/350F/Gas 4.

Drizzle a little oil into the base of the dish. Start by forming a layer of potato slices then a layer of aubergine, then leeks and courgettes. Season well, add the garlic and herbs and then repeat the layers again.

In a saucepan heat the cream and HP Sauce and when warm add the gelatine according to the instructions on the packet. Ladle the HP cream mixture over the vegetables and finally sprinkle the mixed herbs on the top.

Loosely cover with foil, place the dish in the centre of the oven and cook for 20 minutes. Remove the foil and return to the oven for a further 15 minutes until the top coating is golden brown.

Serve hot as it is or press the top down gently with a spatula and leave the dish to cool – it will then easily cut into thick slices when thoroughly cold. Perfect for lunches, picnics and parties.

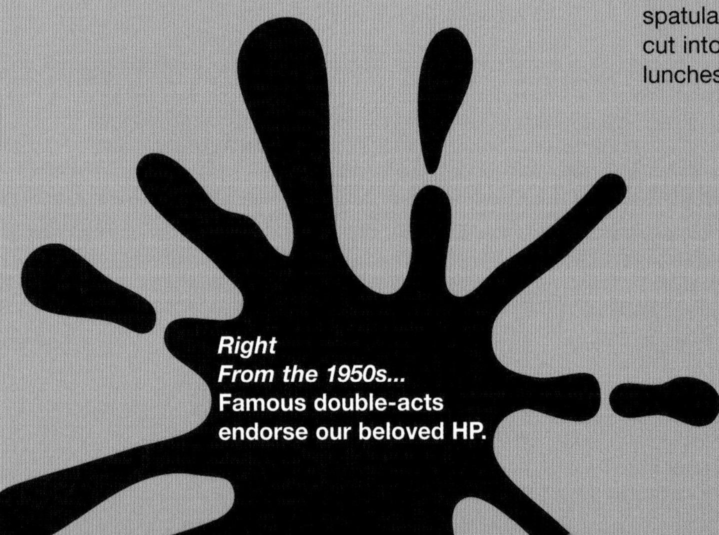

Right
From the 1950s...
Famous double-acts endorse our beloved HP.

Lenny the Lion: If I was a real lion I would insist on having my lion-tamers dished up with H.P. Sauce. *Everything* goes with H.P. Sauce.

Terry Hall: If you were a real lion you wouldn't get the chance – *I'd* bag the lion's share of the H.P. Sauce. You wouldn't dip a whisker in this H.P. Tomato Ketchup either. I love it – it's so rich in tomato ! Like you and me, Lenny, H.P. Sauce and Tomato Ketchup are a really . . .

Happy Pair!

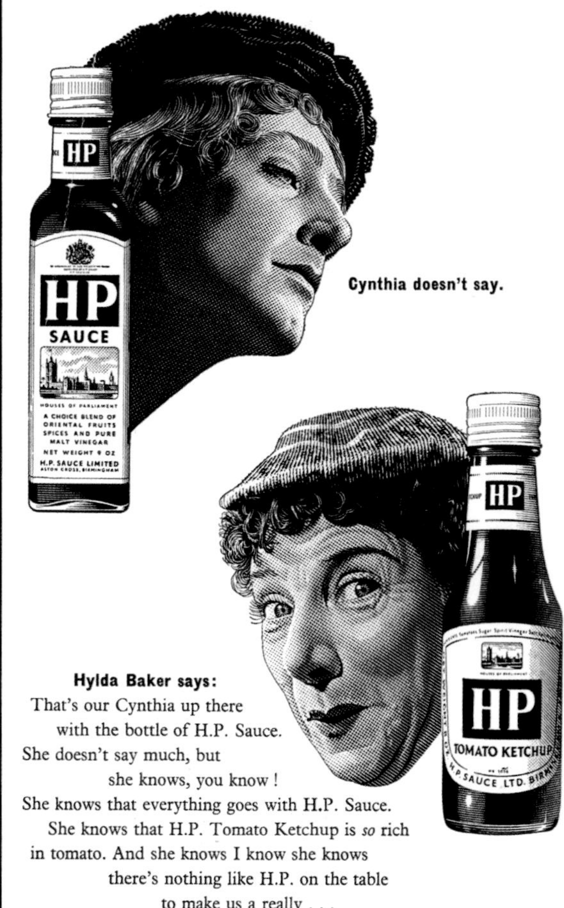

Cynthia doesn't say.

Hylda Baker says: That's our Cynthia up there with the bottle of H.P. Sauce. She doesn't say much, but she knows, you know ! She knows that everything goes with H.P. Sauce. She knows that H.P. Tomato Ketchup is *so* rich in tomato. And she knows I know she knows there's nothing like H.P. on the table to make us a really . . .

Happy Pair!

She knows, you know!

CRAB CLAWS WITH GINGER & CORIANDER

This is a real 'get involved' dish. Crack the crab shells, enjoy the sweet meat and savour the delicious fresh tastes.

SERVES 4 AS A STARTER

1 tablespoon sesame oil
100g thinly sliced shallots
2 cloves garlic, finely chopped
1 tablespoon fresh ginger, peeled and finely diced
1 heaped teaspoon hot chilli flakes
2 tablespoons HP Sauce
2 tablespoons runny honey
1 tablespoon fish sauce
16 crab claws
chopped fresh coriander, to serve
wedges of lime, to serve
sourdough bread, to serve

Sprinkle a little oil into a wok over a medium heat and when it's hot add the shallots, garlic and ginger and stir-fry for 3–4 minutes with a pinch of salt.

Remove the wok from the heat and add the chilli flakes, stir in the HP, honey and fish sauce and then return to the heat. When the mixture is bubbling toss in the crab claws and turn them to coat heating the claws through for 2–3 minutes.

Tip out onto serving plates, scatter with coriander, add wedges of lime and warm chunks of sourdough bread.

What a blessing that eggs are such good value at this time of year. There are so many satisfying meals to make with them – that are really easy too! And eggs are so much more exciting, when you add a drop of HP to the recipe. The pure flavour of finest tomatoes in HP Tomato Ketchup. The rich flavour of blended fruits and spices in HP Sauce. Who else but HP gives you so much goodness?

6 beat-the-clock ways with eggs & HP*

Buttered Eggs

4 rashers streaky bacon
1 oz butter or margarine
1 tablespoon HP Tomato Ketchup
2 eggs

Cut streaky rashers in half and put 4 halves each into 2 individual ovenproof dishes. Cream the butter or margarine with the HP Tomato Ketchup. Break an egg over bacon in each dish. Top with the butter and ketchup mixture. Bake in a fairly hot oven for 10 minutes, or until egg is set. Add a dash of HP Sauce on it – makes a marvellous quick snack.

Blushing Rarebit

4 oz grated cheese
1 tablespoon HP Tomato Ketchup
½ oz butter or margarine
2 slices bread
2 eggs

Put grated cheese, HP Tomato Ketchup and butter or margarine into small thick saucepan. Melt mixture gradually, stirring over low heat. Toast bread slices, and spread thickly with hot cheese mixture. Put under grill until golden brown. Poach eggs until set. Top each hot rarebit with a poached egg. Serve with HP Sauce on it – delicious!

Stuffed Eggs

4 eggs
HP Tomato Ketchup

Hard boil eggs, allowing 2 for each person. Cut eggs in half, putting yolks into bowl. Mash yolks with 1 tablespoon HP Tomato Ketchup until soft. Refill egg halves, and serve with salad, and to top it all, HP Sauce – marvellous!

Egg Pasties

½ lb. short pastry
Filling:
2 hard-boiled eggs
2 skinned pork sausages
or ¼ lb. sausage meat
1 tablespoon HP Tomato Ketchup
1 teaspoon chopped parsley
salt and pepper

Filling: chop hard-boiled eggs, put in a bowl with sausage meat, HP Tomato Ketchup, parsley and seasoning. Blend thoroughly.
Roll pastry thinly into a square. Cut in four. Divide filling in four and put a portion on each pastry square. Damp edges and fold into a triangle, sealing edges firmly. Put on a greased baking sheet, brush with a little milk and bake at 400°F. – Gas 6 for 10 minutes. Reduce heat to 350°F. – Gas 3-4 and cook for a further 15 minutes. Serve hot or cold with HP Sauce on it.

Zippy Popovers

2 oz flour
pinch of salt
pinch of cayenne pepper
1 egg
1 tablespoon HP Sauce
5 tablespoons milk
1 tablespoon finely chopped onion
2 tablespoons grated cheese
HP Tomato Ketchup

Sift flour with seasonings into bowl, hollow out the centre and drop in egg and 3 tablespoons of the milk. Beat with wooden spoon, gradually drawing in flour from basin sides and adding rest of milk to make smooth batter. Stir in HP Sauce, chopped onion and grated cheese.
Divide cooking fat between 12 patty tins and put in hot oven (450°F. – Gas 8) until fat is very hot, remove from oven. Give batter a stir, then divide between tins. Put back in oven and cook for about 15 minutes or until well risen and golden brown. Serve hot with HP Tomato Ketchup on it!

Portuguese Omelet

1 onion
1 tomato
almonds
few sultanas
seasoning, herbs
a little oil
HP Tomato Ketchup

Chop an onion finely, and cook until transparent in oil. Add a chopped tomato, a few chopped almonds, a few sultanas, seasoning and herbs. Blend when cooked with a tablespoon HP Tomato Ketchup.
Make a 3-egg omelet, fold and pour hot onion and tomato mixture over, topping with a very little finely grated cheese, and a final touch of HP Sauce. Fabulous!

***HP – in it and on it! HP Sauce, HP Tomato Ketchup**

LAMB & MINT PASTIES

Pasties are a traditional lunch snack served by farmers wives to the lads working the land. This recipe has retained all the ingredients, flavours and delight of a pasty fresh from the farmhouse oven.

MAKES 6 PASTIES

450g lamb, cut into 1cm cubes
150g potatoes
75g carrots
100g of turnip and swede mixed
1 large onion, roughly chopped
½ teaspoon dried thyme
1 teaspoon good ready-made mint sauce
1½ tablespoons HP Sauce
salt and pepper
1kg pack of readymade short crust pastry
1 dessertspoon sunflower oil
1 free-range egg
1 tablespoon fresh milk

Pour the sunflower oil into a large saucepan adding the onion. Cook over a medium heat until the onion is transparent but not coloured.

Add the lamb to the onion. Continue to cook until all the lamb is sealed, this should take about 10 minutes. Keeping the same heat add the thyme, HP Sauce, a pinch of salt and a very generous grind of black pepper – pasties need pepper!

When the lamb is approaching tender, after about 30–40 minutes, add the remaining vegetables and the mint sauce and mix all together well in the pan. Continue to cook until the vegetable pieces are just softening. Test the mixture and adjust the seasoning to your taste, set aside to cool.

Roll out the short crust pastry to a little under ½ cm thick on a clean cool, well floured surface. Lay a small plate, ideally 20cm diameter, over the pastry and cut round it. Remove the excess pastry. Brush around the edge of the pastry circle with cold water. Place 140g of the lamb mix into the centre and bring the top and the bottom of the circle together over the mixture pinching it together to make a 2cm joint from side to side. Fold 1cm of pastry over the end. Now here is the clever bit, using your thumb and fore finger squeeze the pastry joint together and crimp it all along the edge until it looks like a traditional pasty. Brush the outside with a half-and-half beaten-egg-and-milk mixture. This will give the cooked pasty a lovely golden sheen.

Place the made pasties on baking parchment on a flat tray and cook at 180C/350F/Gas 4 for the first 15 minutes reducing to 150C/300F/Gas 2 for another 12 minutes. Remove from the oven and place on a cooling tray for the pastry to set.

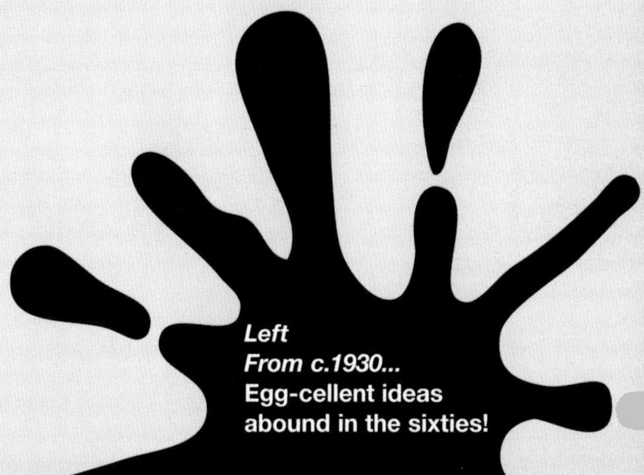

Left
From c.1930...
Egg-cellent ideas abound in the sixties!

HP SA

- always
with Fish

Nº 319/2

Left
From c.1930...
It's fine for fish!

PHEASANT WITH DATE & RED WINE SAUCE

If you're lucky enough to live in the country, a brace of pheasant in the season costs very little so this can be a simple and inexpensive dish with serious style.

SERVES 2

1 oven ready pheasant
1 tablespoon olive oil
500ml chicken stock
200ml red wine
2 tablespoons port
2 tablespoons HP Sauce
250g dates, halved and stoned
salt and freshly ground black pepper

Preheat the oven to 200C/400F/Gas 6.

Using a sharp knife or a pair of poultry shears cut the pheasant in half down the centre and then cut each half into 2 equal portions.

Place the pheasant pieces in a large bowl. Drizzle the olive oil over them and with your hands make sure the meat is all lightly coated. Season with salt and freshly ground black pepper.

Heat a dry heavy-based frying pan. Add the pheasant pieces and sauté to colour. Turn them over and when the pieces are browned, place them in a deep roasting pan skin side down.

Put the stock, wine, port and HP Sauce into a saucepan and bring to the boil. Pour the liquid over the pheasant. Put the roasting pan in the oven and cook uncovered for 30 minutes, turning the pheasant to skin side up half way through to crisp it. Add the dates at this stage.

Remove from the oven and lift out the pheasant portions and dates, keep warm and rest for 15 minutes. Put the roasting tin on the top of the stove, turn up the heat to high and reduce the gravy to a thick sauce, this will take about 5 minutes.

Arrange the pheasant portions and dates on warmed serving plates and pour over the rich sauce.

Doctor Alfred Hill was the first head of Birmingham's Health Department, and served as a public analyst,

GUJERATI MANGO & LENTIL CURRY

An inspired vegetarian curry that even if you're not a vegetarian will float your boat all the way to India!

SERVES 4

$^1/_2$ teaspoon cumin seeds
$^1/_2$ teaspoon black mustard seeds
2 cloves of garlic, crushed
1 onion, peeled and chopped
$^1/_2$ teaspoon salt
1 tablespoon vegetable oil
1 tablespoon brown sugar
250g red lentils, soaked overnight in water, rinsed and drained
4 tablespoons HP Sauce
2 chillies, finely chopped
$^1/_2$ teaspoon turmeric
400ml vegetable stock
2 large ripe mangoes, peeled and cubed

Dry fry the cumin and mustard seeds in a small pan until they begin to pop and lightly colour, releasing their wonderful aroma, then tip them into a pestle and mortar and grind them to fully unleash their flavour.

Put the ground spices together with the garlic, onion and salt into a blender and process to a paste. Heat the oil in a heavy based pan and add the paste, cooking over a gentle heat and stirring all the time until it just begins to brown.

Add the sugar, lentils, HP, chillies and turmeric together with the stock, bring up to the boil and then simmer for 20 minutes. Toss in the mango chunks and cook for a further 10 minutes until you have a thick rich sauce.

Serve with chapatti or naan breads.

new century still hung thick in the air, his endorsement for the company's newest product sounded like a bell-ring of joy, proudly announcing the arrival of a very special sauce: 'I beg to report that I have analysed the sample of Garton's H.P. Sauce and find it to be made from the best materials. The well-known Midland Vinegar Company's vinegar, than which in my opinion there is no better, is used in its preparation. It is of a pleasant and piquant flavour and is in every respect a THOROUGHLY GOOD SAUCE.' It was 1903. Thousands of green glass bottles of the sauce adorned the windows of food stores across the nation. Hill had had his say, now the public would have theirs. **READ ON.... p44**

BRUNCH WRAP

Eat in, take out, hot or cold – this makes a perfect on-the-go brunch.

MAKES 4 WRAPS

500g puff pastry (defrosted if frozen)
4 tablespoons HP Sauce
4 rashers streaky bacon, lightly grilled
100g tin of baked beans
4 small tomatoes, sliced
2 eggs, hardboiled and sliced
2 pork sausages, cooked
freshly milled black pepper
milk for brushing

Pre-heat the oven to 190C/375F/Gas 5.

On a lightly floured surface roll out the pastry to about ½ cm thick and cut out 4 x 16cm squares. Take each piece with the 4 points like a compass facing north, south, east and west. Roll out the east and west sides so that you have an elongated diamond – these will be wrapping over the filling. Spread each piece of pastry with a tablespoon of HP Sauce.

Now for the filling. Lay first a rasher of bacon in each top to bottom, then a spoon of beans spread out, then slices of tomatoes, then the egg and finally half a sausage cut lengthways. Season with pepper.

Take each one and fold the larger flaps into the centre over the filling. Seal with a little water. Brush with a little milk and place on a baking tray lined with parchment. Bake in the centre of the oven for 15 minutes until the wraps are puffy and golden. Leave to rest a few minutes before serving.

CALF'S LIVER & PANCETTA WITH CARAMELISED RED ONIONS

This combination of finely textured pan-fried liver, wafer-thin pancetta and sweet red onions makes a stunning informal supper party dish.

FOR 4 FRIENDS

40g butter
1 large red onion, thinly sliced
½ tablespoon Demerara sugar
1 tablespoon red wine vinegar
salt and black pepper
12 rashers pancetta (or streaky bacon)
600g calf's liver, thinly sliced
2 tablespoons HP Sauce
freshly chopped parsley

First, caramelise the onions. In a pan melt half the butter and cook the onions until softened. Now add the sugar, red wine vinegar and season with salt and pepper. Cover and cook for 10 minutes over a low heat until caramelised.

Pop the pancetta under a medium grill until its just getting crispy around the edges, remove and roughly dice.

Season the liver with salt and pepper. Using a frying pan, heat the remaining butter until it begins to bubble and then slide in the liver. The object here is to brown the outside and still leave the liver pink inside, which should take no more than 2 minutes on each side. Stack the liver to one side of the pan, add the HP Sauce, the pancetta and the caramelised onions and quickly mix together. You don't want to cook the liver any longer than is necessary.

Serve as a stack with the caramelised onions on top and a flourish of freshly chopped parsley.

MIDDLE EASTERN HOT PEPPER DIP

This wonderful dip is my version of the *Muhamarra* found in the Middle East in which the spice blend in HP Sauce really adds an exotic twist.

SERVES 6

1 large red pepper
3 cloves garlic, peeled
½ teaspoon salt
1 onion, finely diced
70g fresh white breadcrumbs
50g walnuts, toasted under a grill for 3–4 minutes and finely chopped
1 tablespoon fresh lemon juice
2 tablespoons HP Sauce
1 teaspoon ground cumin
1 teaspoon chilli powder
150ml olive oil
warmed pitta bread, to serve
mint leaves, to garnish

Char the pepper under a hot grill or over a flame using a pair of tongs. Pop it into a paper bag and close. Leave for 5 minutes and then you will find the skin easy to remove from the soft flesh. Discard any seeds and pith and roughly chop the pepper, then pop it into a food processor.

Chop the garlic roughly on a board and mash with the salt to make a paste. Add this to the processor together with the onion, breadcrumbs, walnuts, lemon juice, HP Sauce, cumin and chilli. Blend all these ingredients together until you have a smooth paste. Now gradually add the olive oil, with the blender still going.

Transfer the pepper dip to a bowl and serve at room temperature with warm pitta bread and mint leaves. This dip is also great with kebabs, grilled meat and fish.

SPLAT STAT

THE ASTON FACTORY THAT WAS HOME TO HP SAUCE FOR SO MANY YEARS WAS UNIQUE IN THAT THE SITE WAS DIVIDED BY THE A38(M) MOTORWAY. A PIPELINE WAS USED TO CARRY VINEGAR FROM ONE SIDE OF THE FACTORY ABOVE SEVEN LANES OF THE ASTON EXPRESSWAY AND OVER TO THE OTHER! IN THE 1970S, THE PIPELINE LEAKED, DAMAGING THE PAINTWORK OF THE PASSING TRAFFIC BELOW!

OXTAIL SOUP

Oxtail is gloriously rich when slow cooked and mixed with vegetables and herbs. Here is a soup with a long heritage justly deserving a well earned revival.

SERVES 6

1kg oxtail, trimmed and cut into pieces
25g unsalted butter
½ tablespoon olive oil
2 stalks celery, chopped
1 onion, diced, skin on
1 small turnip, diced
1 carrot, diced
500ml beef stock
3 tablespoons HP Sauce
6 peppercorns
2 cloves
small piece of mace
small bunch herbs
salt and black pepper
1 tablespoon sherry

Brown the oxtail in the butter and oil in a large casserole pan. Add the vegetables, the stock, HP Sauce and 1 litre of water. Bring to the boil adding the peppercorns, cloves, mace and herbs. Season with salt and freshly ground black pepper.

Cover the casserole, turn the heat down to a simmer and cook for 2½ hours until the meat is really tender and falling away from the bones.

Allow to cool a little and then strain the whole lot through a colander or sieve into a suitable bowl. Cover the liquid and chill in the fridge for 1 hour. Discard the vegetables and bones together with any fat or skin from the oxtail, leaving you with just the meat. Break this up into small pieces and set aside.

When the liquid has chilled you will be able to easily skim off any fat on the surface. Put the remaining jellied juices into a saucepan and if it needs to be thicker bring to the boil and reduce until you have the desired consistency. Add in the meat and cook for 5 minutes then check the seasoning. Remove from the heat, stir in the sherry and serve.

A SAUCE OF HAUTE QUALITÉS... ...A KIND OF FRENCH PRIMER

SINGAPORE PEANUT NOODLES

Noodles make a great base for so many dishes. Cook noodles this way adding your favourite vegetables, meat or fish for the perfect fast food – but with real depth of flavour.

SERVES 2–4

100g Chinese dried medium egg noodles (or 200g fresh noodles)
2 tablespoons sesame oil
1 bunch spring onions, sliced
1 teaspoon freshly grated ginger
3 tablespoons peanut butter
2 tablespoons HP Sauce
1 teaspoon sugar
1 teaspoon chilli flakes
100ml vegetable stock
100g fresh beansprouts
50g roasted, unsalted peanuts, crushed

Put the egg noodles into a pan of boiling water, cover and remove from the heat for about 5 minutes while the noodles rehydrate.

In a wok or large frying pan heat the sesame oil, add the onions and ginger and cook over a gentle heat until tender. Stir in the peanut butter, HP Sauce, sugar, chilli flakes and stock and combine over the heat for 2–3 minutes.

Swizzle the noodles with a fork to loosen them and then drain. Tip the beansprouts into the wok, turning them in the sauce for a couple of minutes and then add in the noodles and toss the whole lot together. Tip out onto a warm serving dish and scatter with the crushed peanuts.

As well as being a great vegetarian option you can also add prawns, cooked chicken or pork and it's a great way of using up leftovers. Simply add them at the same time as you stir in the peanut butter.

In September 1914, the Great War had begun and an uncertainty and gloom hung over the country. For the first time in the company's history, women took up positions in the factory, as the male workforce left to go and fight for their country. The wives and girlfriends helped maintain production and ensured that supplies of HP could be sent out to the troops. Indeed, it was said that a smattering of HP was all that made the soldiers' rations of bully beef bearable! And it was towards the end of the war that Moore introduced to the HP label what would become for many British children their first education in foreign language: the famous paragraph exclaiming the wonders of HP Sauce, written in French. Some thought it a tribute to our allies in the war; others assumed it a nod to the vast quantity of sauce devoured by the troops in France. It was, in fact, a clever attempt to 'upmarket' the sauce and align it with the splendours of French cuisine.

READ ON... p56

SAUCE

Cette sauce de premier choix possède les plus hautes qualités digestives.

C'est un assortiment de fruits d'Orient, d'épices et de Vinaigre de "Malt" pur.

Elle est absolument pure, appétissante et délicieuse avec les viandes chaudes ou froides.

POISSON,
JAMBON,
FROMAGE,
SALADE, &c.,

et pour relever le goût des

SOUPES,
HACHIS,
RAGOÛTS, &c.

SEULS FABRICANTS:

THE MIDLAND VINEGAR Co LIMITED
LONDRES ET BIRMINGHAM.

This Label is also protected under the Trade Marks Acts in Great Britain and many other countries.

E
42

SAUCE

Certificate of Purity

This sauce is free from artificial colouring and preservatives and conforms with pure food laws throughout the world.

It is made from fruits and spices of the highest quality, blended with pure malt vinegar of our own brewing.

All ingredients are regularly tested and examined for quality and purity in our own laboratories and the whole manufacture is under strict analytical control.

As an independent assurance of purity, samples of **H.P. SAUCE** are regularly taken for analysis by Messrs. Bostock Hill & Rigby, Public Analysts and Consulting Chemists.

THE MIDLAND VINEGAR Co LIMITED
LONDON AND BIRMINGHAM.

This Label is also protected under the Trade Marks Acts in Great Britain and many other countries.

SAUCE

HOUSES OF PARLIAMENT

IS A COMBINATION OF THE CHOICEST

ORIENTAL FRUITS SPICES AND PURE MALT VINEGAR

BLENDED WITH THE UTMOST CARE TO ENSURE A

DIGESTIVE RELISH

EVEN FOR THE MOST FICKLE APPETITE, THIS OBJECT HAVING BEEN ATTAINED BY YEARS OF PRACTICAL EXPERIENCE IN THE SAUCE TRADE.

MANUFACTURED BY SOLE PROPRIETORS-

THE MIDLAND VINEGAR Co LIMITED
LONDON AND BIRMINGHAM.

E
42

This Label is also protected under the Trade Marks Acts in Great Britain and many other countries.

SAUCE

Cette sauce de premier choix possède les plus hautes qualités digestives.

C'est un assortiment de fruits d'Orient, d'épices et de Vinaigre de "Malt" pur.

Elle est absolument pure, appétissante et délicieuse avec les viandes chaudes ou froides.

POISSON,
JAMBON,
FROMAGE,
SALADE, &c.,

et pour relever le goût des

SOUPES,
HACHIS,
RAGOÛTS, &c.

SEULS FABRICANTS:

THE MIDLAND VINEGAR Co LIMITED
LONDRES ET BIRMINGHAM.

GARTON'S HP

MARQUE DÉPOSÉE

SAUCE

Cette sauce de premier choix possède les plus hautes qualités digestives.

C'est un assortiment de fruits d'Orient, d'épices et de Vinaigre de "Malt" pur.

Elle est absolument pure, appétissante et délicieuse avec les viandes chaudes ou froides.

This Label is also protected under the Trade Marks Acts in Great Britain and many other countries.

REGD U.S. PAT. OFF.

SAUCE

Certificate of Purity

This sauce is free from artificial colouring and preservatives and conforms with pure food laws throughout the world.

It is made from fruits and spices of the highest quality, blended with pure malt vinegar of our own brewing.

This Label is also protected under the Trade Marks Acts in Great Britain and many other countries.

REGD TRADE MARK.

SAUCE

HOUSES OF PARLIAMENT

IS A COMBINATION OF THE CHOICEST

This Label is also protected under the Trade Marks Acts in Great Britain and many other countries.

MARQUE DÉPOSÉE

SAUCE

Cette sauce de premier choix possède les plus hautes qualités digestives.

C'est un assortiment de fruits d'Orient, d'épices et de Vinaigre de "Malt" pur.

Elle est absolument pure, appétissante et délicieuse avec les viandes chaudes

SAUCE

ertificate of Purity

is sauce is free from arti-
colouring and preservatives
onforms with pure food
hroughout the world.

is made from fruits and
of the highest quality,
d with pure malt vinegar
own brewing.

ingredients are regularly
nd examined for quality
rity in our own labora-
nd the whole manufac-
under strict analytical

n independent assurance
, samples of **H.P. SAUCE**
arly taken for analysis by
Bostock Hill & Rigby,
nalysts and Consulting
Chemists.

LAND VINEGAR Co
LIMITED
LONDON
AND
RMINGHAM.

REGD TRADE MARK.

SAUCE

HOUSES OF PARLIAMENT

IS A COMBINATION OF
THE CHOICEST
ORIENTAL FRUITS
SPICES AND
PURE MALT VINEGAR
BLENDED WITH THE UTMOST
CARE TO ENSURE A
DIGESTIVE RELISH
EVEN FOR THE MOST FICKLE APPETITE.
THIS OBJECT HAVING BEEN ATTAINED
BY YEARS OF PRACTICAL EXPERIENCE
IN THE SAUCE TRADE.

MANUFACTURED BY
SOLE PROPRIETORS-

THE MIDLAND VINEGAR Co
LIMITED
LONDON
AND
BIRMINGHAM.

This Label is also protected under the Trade Marks Acts in Great Britain and many other countries.

E
42

MARQUE DÉPOSÉE

SAUCE

Cette sauce de premier choix possède les plus hautes qualités digestives.

C'est un assortiment de fruits d'Orient, d'épices et de Vinaigre de "Malt" pur.

Elle est absolument pure, appétissante et délicieuse avec les viandes chaudes ou froides.

POISSON,
JAMBON,
FROMAGE,
SALADE, &c.,

et pour relever le goût des

SOUPES,
HACHIS,
RAGOÛTS, &c.

SEULS FABRICANTS:

THE MIDLAND VINEGAR Co
LIMITED
LONDRES
ET
BIRMINGHAM.

REGD U.S. PAT. OFF.

SAUCE

Certificate of Purity

This sauce is free from artificial colouring and preservatives and conforms with pure food laws throughout the world.

It is made from fruits and spices of the highest quality, blended with pure malt vinegar of our own brewing.

All ingredients are regularly tested and examined for quality and purity in our own laboratories and the whole manufacture is under strict analytical control.

As an independent assurance of purity, samples of **H.P. SAUCE** are regularly taken for analysis by Messrs. Bostock Hill & Rigby, Public Analysts and Consulting Chemists.

THE MIDLAND VINEGAR Co
LIMITED
LONDON
AND
BIRMINGHAM.

This Label is also protected under the Trade Marks Acts in Great Britain and many other countries.

REGD TRADE

SAU

HOUSES OF PAR

IS A COMBINATI
THE CHOICE
ORIENTAL FI
SPICES AN
PURE MALT VI
BLENDED WITH THE U
CARE TO ENSURE
DIGESTIVE RE
EVEN FOR THE MOST FICKLE
THIS OBJECT HAVING BEEN A
BY YEARS OF PRACTICAL EXP
IN THE SAUCE TRADE.

MANUFACTURED B
SOLE PROPRIETORS

THE MIDLAND VIN
LIMITED
LONDON
AND
BIRMINGHA

RTON'S
HP
U.S. PAT. OFF.
AUCE

ate of Purity

ce is free from arti-
ng and preservatives
ns with pure food
out the world.

de from fruits and
e highest quality,
pure malt vinegar

GARTON'S
HP
REGD TRADE MARK.
SAUCE

HOUSES OF PARLIAMENT

IS A COMBINATION

This Label is also protected under the Tra
and many other co

GARTON'S
HP
MARQUE DÉPOSÉE
SAUCE

Cette sauce de premier choix possède les plus hautes qualités digestives.

C'est un assortiment de fruits d'Orient, d'épices et de Vinaigre de "Malt" pur.

Elle est absolument pure, appétissante et délicie

This Label is also protected under the T
and many other

GARTON'S

HP
REGD U.S. PAT. OFF.
SAUCE

Certificate of Purity

This sauce is free from artificial colouring and preservatives and conforms with pure food laws throughout the world.

It is made from fruits and spices of the highe

This Label is also protected under the
and many oth

GARTON

HP
REGD TRADE MAR
SAUC

HOUSES OF PARLIAM

CHEESY TORTILLAS WITH RATATOUILLE

Tortillas are such a versatile ingredient. This recipe melts gorgeous, gooey cheese into a gently fried tortilla married to a fresh, crunchy ratatouille.

SERVES 4

$^1/_2$ tablespoon olive oil
1 onion, roughly chopped
1 clove garlic, finely chopped
1 small red pepper, deseeded and roughly chopped
1 small aubergine, skin on and diced into 2cm cubes
1 courgette, skin on and diced into 2cm cubes
1 teaspoon fresh chopped oregano (or $^1/_2$ teaspoon dried oregano)
salt and freshly ground black pepper
2 large tomatoes, skinned and roughly chopped
3 tablespoons HP Sauce
4 flour tortillas
200g grated Cheddar

Start by making the ratatouille. First heat the olive oil in a large frying pan and cook the onions and garlic until just softened, add the diced peppers, aubergine and courgettes and mix well together. Add the oregano, season well with salt and pepper and cook fairly quickly to retain the crunch of vegetables for about 8 minutes. Now add the tomatoes and HP Sauce, stir and cook for a further 2–3 minutes.

Brush a separate frying pan with oil over a medium heat and lay in one tortilla at a time. After a couple of minutes sprinkle with a quarter of the cheese, allow it to melt and then fold the fritatta in half and in half again and remove from the pan to a warm serving plate. Repeat with the other tortillas.

Now spoon oodles of the ratatouille half over the tortilla and half onto the plate and serve.

Give your chips yum, mum.
And your fish.
And shepherd's pie. And sausages. Not to mention cold meat salad. And stew. The lot, in fact.
The fabulous HP Sauce adds taste to it all. Good, rich, spicy taste that makes food a little bit special.
For dad. And the children. And you, dear mum.
The fabulous HP Sauce.
CONTENU
BY APPOINTMENT TO HER MAJESTY THE QUEEN
SUPPLIERS OF H P SAUCE
H P SAUCE LTD
HP
SAUCE

HP STEAK & MUSHROOM JACKETS

Steak, sweet red onion, mushrooms, tangy blue cheese, HP Sauce and crispy skinned baked potatoes – it's enough to send your taste buds into overdrive.

SERVES 4

olive oil
4 baking potatoes
sea salt
1 red onion, sliced
200g sliced closed cup mushrooms
2 tablespoons HP Sauce
100ml beef stock
100ml white wine
1 tablespoon Dijon mustard
good dash Tabasco sauce
400g fillet steak
salt and pepper
100g blue cheese
chopped fresh chives

Left
Sound advice for 60s mums.

Heat the oven to 180C/350F/Gas 4.

Drizzle a little olive oil over the potatoes and then turn the potatoes in your hands to cover them completely in the oil. Place them on a baking tray, sprinkle with sea salt and bake in the oven for 1 hour. The salt and oil will give the potatoes a good crispy skin.

Heat the oil in a pan, add the onions and mushrooms and sauté for 5–6 minutes until softened. Mix together the HP Sauce, stock, wine, mustard and Tabasco and add this to the pan. Cook gently for about 8 minutes until the sauce is thickened.

Meanwhile heat the grill to medium-high, season the steak and cook for approximately 10 minutes depending on how thick it is and how rare you like your steak (for a fillet that is 2.5cm thick, 10 minutes should give you a medium-rare steak). Turn once during cooking. Remove the steak and rest it for 5 minutes, keeping it warm. Cut the steak into slices and add it to the onion and mushroom mixture and stir.

Cut the potatoes with a cross halfway through and then squeeze with fingers and thumbs to open them up. Pack in the steak and mushroom mixture and then sprinkle with crumbled blue cheese and scatter with chopped chives.

BRISKET WITH FIGS & RUM

Beef, cooked long and slow and infused with the sunshine flavours of figs and rum, develops a sensation of taste that brings a whole new experience to the Sunday roast.

SERVES 6

1.5 kg brisket
1 litre good beef stock
1 large onion, peeled and roughly chopped
2 stalks of celery, roughly chopped
2 carrots, peeled and chopped
2–3 sprigs thyme
2 bay leaves
12 black peppercorns
1 tablespoon brown sugar
250g dried figs
100ml rum
2 tablespoons HP Sauce

Put the brisket into a suitable size pan and pour over the stock. Add the vegetables, herbs, peppercorns and sugar and bring up to the boil. Turn down the heat to just simmering and cook covered for 4 hours.

While this is cooking soak the figs in the rum.

Preheat the oven to 180C/350F/Gas 4. Remove the brisket from the liquid and cover and keep warm. Strain the juices from the pan, discarding half the liquid and retaining the vegetables.

Place the brisket in a roasting tin with the vegetables tucked in around it and cook in the oven for 30 minutes after which time the outside will become golden and crispy.

Put the reserved liquid back into a saucepan over a high heat and reduce it down to half again. Add the figs, rum and HP Sauce and simmer for 20 minutes while the meat is finishing in the oven. If the gravy needs further thickening, add a teaspoon of cornflour mixed with an equal amount of water.

Serve thick succulent slices of brisket and vegetables doused with fig and rum gravy.

SPLAT STAT

IT WAS IN 1940, AS A RESULT OF WARTIME RATIONING WHICH CUT THE PRINTED MATTER ON LABELS TO A BARE MINIMUM, THAT THE LINK TO THE RECIPE'S ORIGINAL OWNER, 'GARTON'S', WAS DROPPED FROM THE LABEL, NEVER TO RETURN.

HUNTERS' CHICKEN

This dish gets its name from being traditionally served at the end of a long day's hunting but it's just as good to serve after a long day's hunting round the shops!

SERVES 4–6

1 free-range chicken
salt and black pepper
2 tablespoons olive oil
2 onions, sliced
200g button mushrooms
200ml vermouth or white wine
200ml chicken stock
2 tablespoon tomato purée
3 tablespoons HP Sauce
1 tablespoon chopped fresh tarragon
400g fresh chopped tomatoes
1 tablespoon chopped fresh parsley
crème fraîche, to serve

Preheat the oven to 180C/350F/Gas 4.

Cut the chicken into 10 pieces, including each breast into 2 and the legs in half. Season well with salt and freshly ground black pepper

Heat the oil in a frying pan and brown the chicken pieces for a few minutes. You may need to do this in a couple of batches. Lift the chicken from the pan with a slotted spoon and place in an ovenproof casserole.

Now cook the onions and mushrooms in the same frying pan for 5 minutes, stirring occasionally, until they begin to soften. Add the vermouth, stock, tomato purée and HP Sauce, together with the tarragon and cook for a further 5 minutes, then tip into the casserole with the chicken. Place the casserole in the oven and cook for 1 hour.

Remove from the oven, and skim off any excess oil from the juice. Stir in the tomatoes, return it to the oven and cook uncovered for a further 20 minutes while the sauce reduces. (You can thicken it with a little cornflour mixed with a splash of water, if desired)

Scatter with the parsley and leave to rest for 5 minutes before serving with a swirl of crème fraîche and some good chunky roast potatoes.

ROAST POUSSIN WITH GARLIC & HERBS

Poussin, also known as spring chicken, are enjoyed because they are tender and flavoursome. Here, I have added the dynamics of garlic and herbs to make a really tasty dish.

SERVES 2

2 small heads of garlic, complete and unpeeled
olive oil
salt and fresh black pepper
2 poussin (oven ready)
4 sprigs fresh thyme
4 sprigs fresh rosemary
2 medium potatoes, peeled and sliced
50g unsalted butter, melted
2 tablespoons HP Sauce

Pre-heat the oven to 200C/400F/Gas 6.

Take the 2 heads of garlic and trim across the top taking off about 1cm. Drizzle with a little olive oil, season with plenty of salt and pepper, place in a roasting tin and roast for 15 minutes.

Remove the garlic from the oven and allow them to cool enough to handle. Put one head of garlic into each poussin together with 2 sprigs of each of the herbs. Season the poussin with salt and pepper and put them into the roasting tin. Now tuck the sliced potatoes under and round the poussin in the tin.

Whisk the butter and HP Sauce together and brush it all over the poussins pouring the remainder over the sliced potatoes. Roast in the centre of the hot oven for 40 minutes.

When cooked, remove the poussin, allow to rest for a few minutes and then serve with the golden potatoes and your favourite vegetables.

MAPLE HP RIB CHOPS

This is an inexpensive and easy dish to cook. Wrap your taste buds around succulent pork, maple syrup, a zing of mustard and the deep HP Sauce flavours and this will surely become a favourite for all.

SERVES 4

1kg pork rib chops
1 litre chicken stock
6 tablespoons maple syrup
2 tablespoons brown sugar
2 tablespoons cider vinegar
2 tablespoons HP Sauce
1 heaped teaspoon mustard powder

Put the rib chops into a large saucepan with the stock, adding extra water to cover, and bring to the boil. Turn down the heat to a very gentle simmer, cover and cook for 45–60 minutes until tender.

Drain the ribs, discarding the stock, and put them into a large shallow dish. Warm the syrup, sugar, vinegar, HP Sauce and mustard powder in a pan for 5 minutes. Remove from the heat and pour the syrupy mixture over the ribs, turning them and making sure they are well coated. Allow to cool and then pop in the fridge for 2–3 hours to marinate.

When the barbecue is in full swing and the coals at perfect cooking temperature lay on the ribs and cook for 10 minutes, basting with any remaining marinade, or until the ribs are golden brown and ready to devour. If you haven't got a barbecue these will cook perfectly on a griddle on the stove.

HAROLD'S PREFERENCE

In 1964, a casual remark did more to pique interest in HP Sauce than the marketing-campaign or selling-strategy dreams of any company executive of the era could have wished for. A new government had been elected to power, led by Harold Wilson. He was …

STUFFED BUTTERNUT SQUASH

This dish has great flavour matched with great texture. The cider and HP Sauce lifts all the vegetables to tasty highs and the garlic and chilli give it an extra bite.

SERVES 4

2 small butternut squash
2 tablespoons olive oil
celery salt and freshly milled black pepper
1 small red chilli, finely diced
2 cloves garlic, finely chopped
200g chestnut mushrooms, sliced
100ml dry cider
3 tablespoons HP Sauce
400g tin cannellini beans, drained
2 tablespoons chopped flat leaf parsley, to garnish

Heat the oven to 180C/350F/Gas 4.

Cut the butternut squash in half lengthways without removing the skin and scoop out the seeds. Brush the flesh with a little of the olive oil and season with salt and pepper. Put the squash in a baking tin, cover with foil and roast for 45–60 minutes, depending on the size, until they are soft all the way through.

Heat the remaining oil in a pan and gently fry the chilli, garlic and mushrooms for 3–4 minutes. Add the cider, HP Sauce and beans, season with celery salt and black pepper and simmer for a further 5 minutes, or until the juices have reduced down, and then stir in a good tablespoon of chopped parsley.

When the squash is cooked place one half on each plate and fill with the beany mixture spooning any remaining on the side. Scatter with the remaining parsley.

to the question of whether her husband had any bad habits, she quipped that if he did have a fault it was that he drowned everything she cooked in HP Sauce! This was publicity on an unprecedented scale; the media leapt on the comment, and her words were widely satirised by columnists and commentators of the day. The Prime Minister decided neither to confirm nor refute the statement. After all, a preference for the sauce suggested that he was a man of the people, a man of popular tastes! HP Sauce's connections with the Houses of Parliament now seemed irrefutable. It wasn't until 1975, on the occasion of the centenary celebration of the Midland Vinegar Company, with the renowned fan of the sauce as the Company's guest of honour, that the former Prime Minister revealed that his wife's innocent remark from over a decade ago was inaccurate only so much as it wasn't HP Sauce for which he had a particular penchant, but Worcestershire Sauce! He left the company assembled there dumbfounded, but the myth prevailed. **READ ON** p64

HP SA

- always with Cheese

Left
From c.1930...
It's champion with cheese!

HONEY-GRILLED SALMON WITH KIWI & CUCUMBER SALSA

This is a dish with great colour – the pink salmon and the fresh green salsa enthusiastically matched with a delicious sweet and sour explosion of flavours.

SERVES 4

2 tablespoons HP Sauce
1 teaspoon Dijon mustard
2 tablespoons runny honey
1 tablespoon sesame oil
4 salmon fillets (approximately 200g each)
salt and pepper

For the salsa
2 tablespoons lime juice
1 tablespoon runny honey
2 firm kiwi fruits, peeled and diced
$^1/_4$ cucumber, unpeeled and finely diced
$^1/_2$ green pepper, deseeded and finely diced
1 small onion, finely chopped
1 small green chilli, deseeded and finely diced
2 heaped tablespoons fresh coriander, chopped

In a small bowl mix together the HP Sauce, mustard, honey and sesame oil. Brush the salmon fillets with this mixture, season with salt and pepper and leave in the fridge for 30 minutes.

Combine the lime juice and honey in a bowl and toss in the kiwi, cucumber, green pepper, onion, chilli and coriander turning them all in the juices. Leave this covered at room temperature while the salmon marinates.

Heat the grill to medium high and cook the fillets for 8–10 minutes, depending on the thickness, basting more mixture over them as they cook.

Serve the salmon with the salsa piled on top.

LAMB TAGINE WITH PRUNES, OLIVES & ALMONDS

This is a dish originating from Morocco and begging to be shared. Although the ingredients should really come from the busy, noisy, bustling street markets, if you can't make Marrakesh the supermarket will suffice.

SERVES 4–6

For the tagine spice mix
1 tablespoon ground ginger
1 tablespoon ground black pepper
1 tablespoon turmeric
2 teaspoons ground cinnamon
1 teaspoon grated nutmeg

For the tagine
1kg lamb, diced into large chunks
2 tablespoons tagine spice mix
1 tablespoons olive oil
400ml lamb or beef stock
3 tablespoons HP Sauce
1 tablespoon honey
1 tablespoon dark brown sugar
150g ready to eat prunes, stoned
10 green olives, stoned and halved
50g slivered almonds, toasted in a dry frying pan
freshly chopped parsley, to serve

Mix together the tagine spices into an airtight jar. You will have enough to make this recipe at least twice and the spices will keep for a few months.

Put the lamb into a dish and sprinkle the 2 tablespoons of spice mix over the meat, coating it thoroughly, then cover and leave in the fridge for at least 2 hours.

Preheat the oven to 150C/300F/Gas 2. Heat the olive oil in a frying pan, sear the lamb chunks all over in batches and transfer them with a slotted spoon to an ovenproof casserole. Pour in the stock, HP Sauce and honey, cover and cook in the oven for 2 hours.

Remove the casserole from the oven, stir in the sugar, prunes and olives and cook for a further half hour. Remove and rest for 20 minutes before serving scattered with almonds and parsley.

BEEF ON THE BONE WITH CHOP HOUSE BUTTER

This is my friend, uber-chef Mark Hix's, inspired take on grilled steak. It is famously served in his now-legendary Oyster and Chop House restaurant situated alongside Smithfield Market in London.

For the Chop House Butter
2 red onions, peeled, halved and finely chopped
2 teaspoons coarsely ground black pepper
2 tablespoon extra virgin rapeseed oil
splash red wine
1 tablespoon chopped thyme leaves
1 tablespoon freshly grated horseradish
500g butter, at room temperature
1 tablespoon Henderson's relish
2 tablespoons HP Sauce
1 tablespoon Tewksbury Mustard
2 teaspoons Gentleman's Relish
(You can freeze the leftover butter for use another time)

2 x T-Bone steaks, around 350g each

To prepare the butter, gently cook the red onions and black pepper in the rapeseed oil for 1–2 minutes then remove from the heat and mix well with all of the other ingredients.

Roll the butter mixture in cling film or greaseproof into a 3cm cylinder and store in the fridge for at least 20 minutes to firm up.

Season the steaks with a little salt and pepper and brush with vegetable oil.

Heat a griddle pan until smoking, and cook the beef cuts for 3–4 minutes on each side (for medium rare), or until cooked to your liking.

Serve the grilled steaks with two 1cm-thick rounds of the Chop House Butter, melting over each steak.

SPLAT STAT

IN 1940 CAME THE FIRST EVER INSTANCE OF THE CLOSELY GUARDED SECRETS OF THE HP RECIPE LEAVING THE COUNTRY. WITH TRANSATLANTIC JOURNEYS FAR TOO PERILOUS TO SHIP SAUCE TO CANADA, THE RECIPE WAS INSTEAD TRANSLATED INTO CODE AND SENT IN TWO HALVES ACROSS THE OCEAN, WITH THE METHOD FOLLOWING ON IN A THIRD ENVELOPE!

FLORENTINE PASTA

HP Sauce and cream make a magical combination as is reflected in this gorgeous pasta dish enhanced further by the baby leaf spinach.

SERVES 2

1 tablespoons olive oil
1 clove garlic, minced
2 shallots, finely diced
1 tablespoon Marsala wine
2 tablespoons HP Sauce
200ml double cream
100g Parmesan cheese, $^3/_4$ grated and $^1/_4$ left for shavings
100g washed baby leaf spinach, stalks removed
1 tablespoon pine nuts, toasted for 3 minutes in a dry pan
salt and pepper
200g linguine, or your favourite pasta

Heat the oil and butter in a large frying pan and add the garlic and shallots. Cook for 3 minutes until just softened and add the Marsala and HP Sauce. Add the cream and the grated Parmesan, bring up to the boil and then add the spinach. Cover and cook over a low heat until the spinach is just wilted and tender. Season with plenty of freshly ground black pepper.

Cook and drain the pasta and then toss with the creamy spinach mixture. Serve with shavings of Parmesan and the toasted pine nuts.

HAPPY DAYS... A SAUCE
WITH SOME PUNCH

VENISON TARTARE

This is inspired by a recipe I found in the *New York Times* and prepared for delighted guests – now you can do the same!

SERVES 4 – 6

4 shallots, finely diced
2 juniper berries, crushed
1 teaspoon capers, rinsed and finely chopped
1 fresh lime, half for juice and half for garnish
1 tablespoon olive oil
2 cloves garlic, minced
sprig of dill, finely chopped
dash Tabasco sauce
1 teaspoon paprika
salt and freshly ground black pepper
500g fresh venison, loin or fillet preferably
1 large egg yolk
2 level tablespoons HP Sauce
$^1/_2$ teaspoon made English mustard

First make the tartare seasoning by mixing together in a bowl the shallots, juniper, capers, lime juice, olive oil, garlic and dill. Then add the Tabasco, paprika, salt and pepper and mix altogether. Cover and leave in the refrigerator for 6 hours or overnight.

Roughly chop the venison and put in a food processor with the tartare seasoning. Blitz as long as it takes to create a mince, not a paste. Transfer the venison to a bowl and add the egg yolks, HP Sauce and mustard. Mix together well.

Divide the mixture into equal patties, forking the surface to enhance their look and serve with toast triangles and a rocket and watercress salad.

In the 1980s, it fell to a man of the people to sell the sauce of the people. Frank Bruno was establishing himself as one of the world's best boxers and was much loved by the people of Britain. HP had signed Bruno and the commentator with whom he had such a cuddly rapport, Harry Carpenter, to film a commercial for television. The voiceover began: 'How to get on the *wrong* side of Frank Bruno:', and Frank was promptly served with a plate of food to which he responded by scowled. The voiceover then interjected once more: 'How to get on the *right* side of Frank Bruno:', and Frank was duly passed the HP Sauce, after which he broke into a merrily whistled tune of 'Happy Days Are Here Again'. The voiceover concluded, 'Only one sauce can give Frank's favourite foods the necessary punch!' A nation almost certainly nodded in agreement! More than two decades later, you would be hard pressed to find a sauce that delivers a more knockout flavour!

DEVILLED LAMB & APRICOT KEBABS

This is a great dish for all seasons – either served on rice when it will warm the darkest of winter nights or when served with a garden-fresh salad and the kebabs straight from the summer barbecue.

MAKES 4 LARGE KEBABS

2 tablespoons HP Sauce
2 teaspoons wholegrain mustard
1 teaspoon medium curry paste
1 tablespoon runny honey
2 tablespoons lemon juice
1 teaspoon fresh thyme leaves
500g lamb neck fillet
freshly milled black pepper
24 ready-to-eat dried apricots
4 bamboo skewers soaked in water to stop them burning during cooking.

In a bowl mix together the HP sauce, mustard, curry paste, honey, lemon juice and thyme.

Cut the lamb into 1cm thick discs. Season them with plenty of black pepper and toss them into the bowl of marinade. Leave for 1 hour.

Thread the lamb and apricot alternately on the skewers and then pop them under a hot grill or on the barbecue, brushing with any remaining sauce for 8–10 minutes until cooked to your liking. Serve with crispy baked potatoes and a leafy salad.

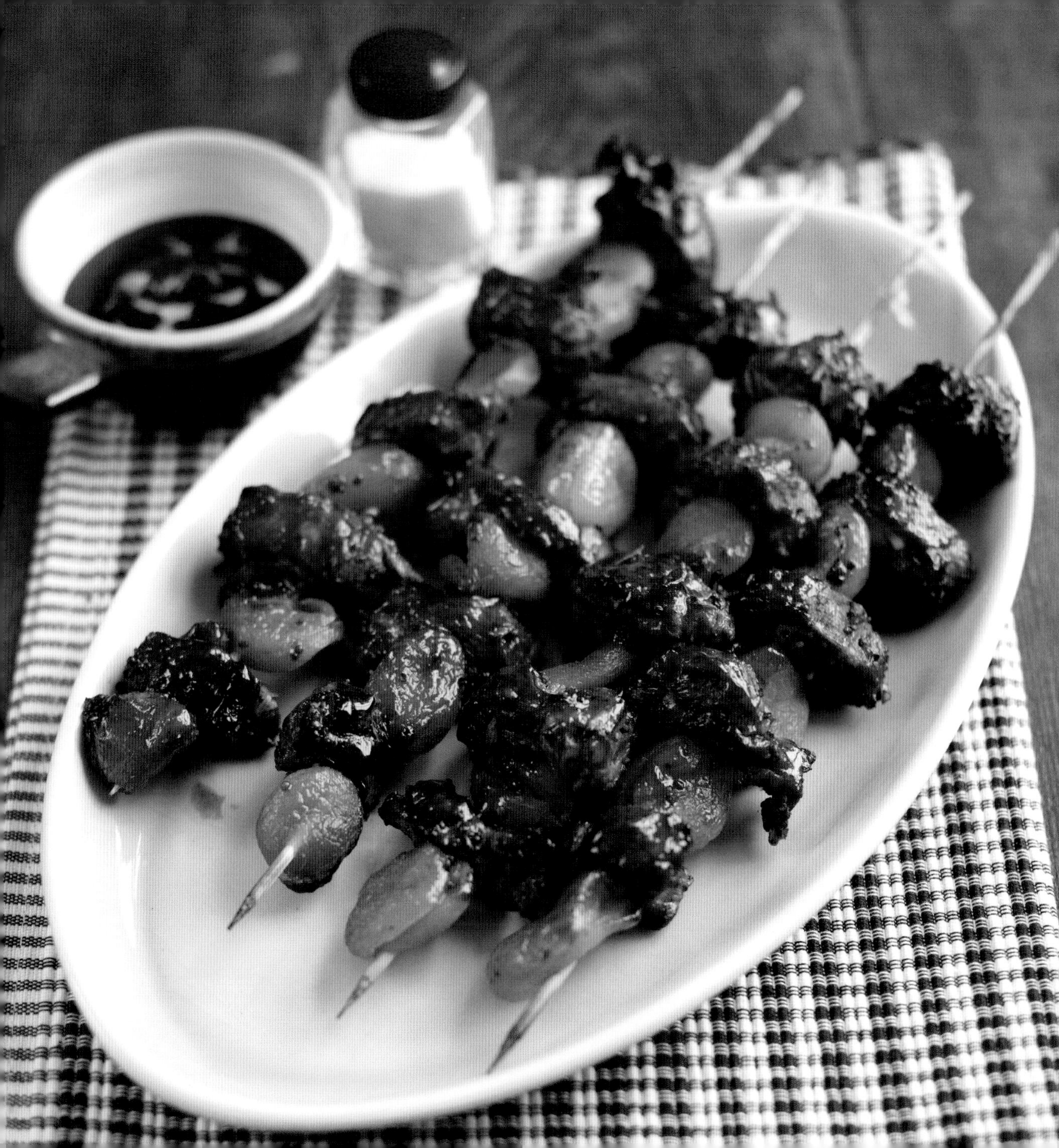

HP HP HP HiP HiP Hooray!
what a saucy pie!
HP
SAUCE

MULLIGATAWNY SOUP

A classic soup of Anglo-Indian origin.

SERVES 6

1 tablespoon vegetable oil
1 onion, chopped
2 cloves garlic, finely chopped
½ teaspoon grated fresh ginger
½ teaspoon chilli powder
pinch ground cinnamon
2 teaspoons curry paste
1 carrot, peeled and chopped
1 apple, peeled, cored and chopped
1 large potato, peeled and diced
200g red lentils, rinsed and drained
1 litre chicken stock
1 tablespoon soft dark brown sugar
2 tablespoons HP Sauce
½ tablespoon lemon juice
1 tin coconut milk

Heat the oil in a large pan and gently cook the onions, garlic and ginger until just turning golden. Add the chilli, cinnamon and curry paste and cook for a further minute.

Next add the carrot, apple, potato, lentils, stock and sugar. Bring to the boil and then simmer gently for 20 minutes so that the vegetables are tender. Remove from the heat and allow to cool a little. Blend in a processor until you have a smooth purée.

Return the purée to the pan and add the HP, lemon juice and coconut milk and reheat for 5 minutes. Great served with warm naan bread and chopped boiled eggs on the side.

Left
A cheeky caption for this late '60s magazine advert.

SPICY ORIENTAL LETTUCE SHELLS

This makes a very pretty starter, simple to make, crispy in texture and packed with flavour.

MAKES 8 STARTER PORTIONS

50g dried cellophane noodles or fine egg noodles
2 tablespoons HP Sauce
1 teaspoon chilli paste
1 teaspoon garlic purée
1 teaspoon five spice powder
1 tablespoon toasted sesame oil
2 tablespoons chopped fresh coriander
150g shredded roast chicken (reclaimed from your Sunday lunch!)
8 nest shaped crispy lettuce leaves (iceberg or similar)

Cover the noodles with boiling water and leave aside for 5 minutes for them to rehydrate. Drain, cool and roughly chop the noodles.

Whisk together the HP Sauce, chilli, garlic, spice and sesame oil until well combined and then add in the coriander.

Into the sauce tip the chicken and noodles and toss well to coat. Divide the chicken mixture between the lettuce leaves so that you can pick them up, roll them up and munch!

HP

MALT
VINEGAR

BRITAIN'S BEST BREW

SHEPHERD'S PIE

This is a great country dish traditionally made to satisfy the hunger of the workers as they came home from the cattle market – and every bit as good today if you've just come home from the Stock Market!

SERVES 4

1 tablespoon vegetable oil
1 onion diced
500g lean minced lamb
1 large carrot
2 sticks celery
400g tin chopped tomatoes
2 sprigs thyme and 1 bay leaf tied together
HP Sauce
1 lamb or beef stock cube
salt and pepper
150g mushrooms, roughly chopped
1 tablespoon plain flour
800g potatoes, peeled
knob of butter
milk
2 teaspoons readymade horseradish sauce

Left
HP Vinegar, from which our HP Sauce story begins!

Heat the oil in a pan and cook the onions until softened. Add in the mince and brown the meat – about 8 minutes – then follow with the carrots and celery. Pour in the tomatoes then add the herbs, HP Sauce, crumble in the stock cube, season well with salt and pepper and cook for 20 minutes over a medium heat.

Add in the mushrooms, sprinkle in the flour and taste the sauce, adjust the seasoning if necessary. Cook for a further 20 minutes by which time you should have a thick, rich, meaty mixture.

Remove from the cooker and leave to cool for 10 minutes. Discard the herb sprig and pour the meat and vegetables, with all the delicious juices, into an ovenproof serving dish with sides at least 5cm high.

Cut the potatoes into roughly even chunks about 5cm square and boil in salted water until cooked, then drain. Mash them until creamy by adding the butter, milk, horseradish and season with pepper. Leave aside to cool a little.

Preheat the oven to 180C/350F/Gas 4. Now gently spread the mashed potato over the lamb and fork it level leaving symmetrical fork lines on top. Bake for 20–30 minutes until your forked mash is golden brown and crispy.

MEXICAN BEEF & BEAN WRAPS

A great looking wrap full of good spicy flavours and textures to keep your troops happy and satisfied at lunchtime.

MAKES 4 WRAPS

1 tablespoon vegetable oil
1 Spanish onion, diced
1 green chilli, finely diced
250g minced lean beef
1 tomato, roughly chopped
1 tablespoon tomato purée
1 tablespoon HP Sauce
salt and pepper
½ tin refried beans, or red kidney beans, drained and rinsed
1 tablespoon chopped oregano
4 flour tortillas
shredded lettuce
1 avocado, peeled, stoned and sliced at the last minute
50g strong Cheddar, grated
sour cream, to serve

Heat the oil in a pan and fry the onions and chilli until soft. Add in the minced beef and cook until browned. Next add the tomato purée and HP Sauce, season with salt and pepper and cook gently for 20 minutes, adding a splash of water if the mixture is too dry.

Stir the beans and oregano into the beef mixture and cook for a further 10–15 minutes, stirring occasionally, as it will be fairly dry.

Warm the tortillas in the oven according to the packet instructions. Onto each tortilla lay some shredded lettuce, a few slices of avocado, a good dollop of beef and beans, a sprinkling of cheese and a spoonful of sour cream. Fold the tortilla first up from the bottom, then wrap over the sides to form an envelope and serve.

REGISTERED
HOUSES OF PARLIAMENT
GARTON'S
H.P.
REGD TRADE MARK.
SAUCE
HOUSES OF PARLIAMENT
IS A COMBINATION OF THE CHOICEST
ORIENTAL FRUITS SPICES AND PURE MALT VINEGAR
BLENDED WITH THE UTMOST CARE TO ENSURE A
DIGESTIVE RELISH
EVEN FOR THE MOST FICKLE APPETITE. THIS OBJECT HAVING BEEN ATTAINED BY YEARS OF PRACTICAL EXPERIENCE IN THE SAUCE TRADE.
MANUFACTURED BY SOLE PROPRIETORS
THE MIDLAND VINEGAR Co LIMITED
LONDON AND BIRMINGHAM.
This Label is also protected under the Trade Marks Acts in Great Britain and many other countries.
HP
GARTON'S
H.P.
SAUCE
HOUSES OF PARLIAMENT
ORIENTAL FRUITS SPICES and
PURE MALT VINEGAR
DIGESTIVE RELISH
MIDLAND VINEGAR Co
BIRMINGHAM

OVER THE DECADES, THE SAUCE MIGHT HAVE CHANGED ITS LOOK, BUT IT REMAINS AS PIQUANT AND PLEASANT AS THE BATCH WHICH FIRST APPEARED ON SHOP SHELVES IN 1903.

WITCH SAUCE?

HP SAUCE...

...OF COURSE!

ACKNOWLEDGEMENTS

Another great sauce and another great series of cooking experiences. My very grateful appreciation goes to the fantastic team at Absolute Press who publish this book. Especially to Jon Croft, who says he doesn't think I'm tricky and that always makes me feel better. Thank you to Matt Inwood whose creative genius always finds new and exciting expression. None of this happens successfully without the help and inspiration of others. As I wrote this book I shared every recipe with my wife Lynda, who shopped, cooked and inspired the whole way through, hinting ideas and adding detail. Lynda, you are such a great asset. Also, thanks to my lovely labrador puppy, Bentley, who barked approval, as we jointly tasted every dish. My grateful thanks also to Andy Jones from the Slab House near the wonderful city of Wells. Andy suggested recipes, and checked the taste and techniques with great encouragement as the book progressed. His contribution is always greatly appreciated. Finally, thank you to Paul Harvey who is at the helm of the HP brand and gave me the privilege of compiling this book.

Images on pages 13, 14, 27, 34, 36, 46, 58, 72 and 76 courtesy of Robert Opie, Museum of Brands, Notting Hill, London.

Images on pages 21, 22, 31, 50 and 68 courtesy of The H.J. Heinz Co. Ltd Archive at The History of Advertising Trust (www.hatads.org.uk).

HP
SAUCE

A HAPPY END?